T0153043

# THRESHOLES

# THRESHOLES

## LARA MIMOSA MONTES

**COFFEE HOUSE PRESS**
Minneapolis
2020

Copyright © 2020 by Lara Mimosa Montes
Cover design by Christina Vang
Book design by Sarah Miner
Author photograph © Rijard Bergeron

Coffee House Press books are available to the trade through our primary distributor, Consortium Book Sales & Distribution, cbsd.com or (800) 283-3572. For personal orders, catalogs, or other information, write to info@coffeehousepress.org.

Coffee House Press is a nonprofit literary publishing house. Support from private foundations, corporate giving programs, government programs, and generous individuals helps make the publication of our books possible. We gratefully acknowledge their support in detail in the back of this book.

LIBRARY OF CONGRESS CATALOGING-IN-PUBLICATION DATA

Names: Mimosa Montes, Lara, author.
Title: THRESHOLES / Lara Mimosa Montes.
Description: Minneapolis : Coffee House Press, 2020.
Identifiers: LCCN 2019028616 (print) | LCCN 2019028617 (ebook) |
    ISBN 9781566895798 (trade paperback) | ISBN 9781566895873
    (ebook)
Classification: LCC PS3613.I5919945 T48 2020 (print) |
    LCC PS3613.I5919945 (ebook) | DDC 818/.609—dc23
LC record available at https://lccn.loc.gov/2019028616
LC ebook record available at https://lccn.loc.gov/2019028617

PRINTED IN THE UNITED STATES OF AMERICA

# PREFACE

This was never the book I intended to write; nevertheless, it is the book that was written. Why did I decide in the writing to turn towards the book before me rather than tighten my grasp on the one that refused to be born? The same reason one might stand in the light of a dead star: to consider the time it took for that light to arrive. This is a story about that story. About the forces inside of an object that push it out into the world, and the ones that threaten to break it apart.

In this way it is also inevitably a story about love and the uncertainty that follows me henceforth. Some days, that unknowing makes me difficult; other days, it makes me odd. On those days, my body hides in the wings so that I can shield my heart from the blowback of a breaking thing.

And when people would ask, "What are you writing?" I would return in response, "It's more like the book is writing me." If this sounds dramatic, it's because it was. My hair fell out, the follicles changed shape, and I could no longer piece together a thought. But to recall Cecilia Vicuña, "A poem only becomes poetry when its structure / is made not of words but forces." During this time, I did not dream about writing. I dreamt about the forces that wished to be written. They were not always generous. Where had I been, and where was I going? Upon revisiting what I had written once, weeks after the fact, I thought in earnest: *Sylvia Plath ain't got shit on me.* It feels blasphemous to say that, but why pretend otherwise, as though my possessiveness did not attach itself to other objects, namely those so full of the nothing by which I felt haunted. Do I need clarity of mind to speak of these forces, or should I regardless? I tried to think through them in every tense I could imagine and put forward what I hoped were not the same old questions.

# THRESHOLES

        ○

        ○

        ○

Once you spoke without an accent
(as if you came
from nowhere).

        ○

Nowhere is not a place.
It is a modulation ..... ..

        ○

A throbbing we carry
Within us; a process, unremitting

        ○

        ○

        ○

It was sequential until it wasn't

        ○

And open to what is adjacent—

        ○

        ○

        ○

In the red notebook I carry always: a blank twenty-five-cent post-
card of Silver Rock, Cannon Beach, Oregon; a small black-and-white

photograph of a cattle crossing taken from behind the dashboard of a car facing the oncoming cattle caravan; and another postcard, featuring an image of the seaside city of Atami, part of Asako Narahashi's series *half awake and half asleep in the water.*

The barren coastal scene captured in the postcard of Silver Rock resembles the beaches of Ingmar Bergman's *The Seventh Seal* and suggests despair of a spiritual origin, while the others, oncoming catastrophe by way of some fatal accident, such as death by stampede or drowning.

I have never, to the best of my recollection, been subject to a Rorschach test, not as a child, nor as an adult, but trust that if there is a life for me to be lived between these images, then these words would be my attempt to describe it.

o

There where the violence is

o

Inside the soft tissue holding

o

Wildflowers like wild parts of me, always desiring

o

An unfolding: to speak of you beyond the rewriting

o

But how without a body

○

○

○

Hearing is the fractality of fragments occurring
(as they disintegrate).  (Mei-mei Berssenbrugge)

○

Daily, I remind myself: the future is not depen-
dent on your inability to describe your undoing.

○

○

○

I had every intention
of beginning were it
not for a narrowing, a tightening.

○

The bands of color in which
I saw myself surrounded;
Beautiful striations, bending

○

The time between rotations

○

And the cut inside language

○

Insofar as that slash produces

○

"I"—a python; a fiction—

○

○

○

I took the shape of what was asked of me like
a wave
that carries the garbage leeward upon the shore

○

Is this an index of the garbage?

○

(Diamond, copper, desert rose)

○

The knowing that takes place outside of a duration

○

And that encounter's relationship to form

○

*Have haunted me episodically as an adult.*

○

In Jack Garfein's Bronx noir, *Something Wild* (1961), Mary Ann experiences a sexual assault at St. James Park, 2550 Jerome Avenue, Bronx, NY 10468, upon leaving the Kingsbridge Road subway station. The film is based on the 1958 novel *Mary Ann,* by Alex Karmel, whose first sentence begins: "One night in March, on her way home from chorus practice, Mary Ann Robinson was raped by an assailant whose features she could not make out in the darkness." The novel revolves around this trauma that Mary Ann cannot in language own. Back in the Bronx, bedridden, I think about the conditions that led me here, to this moment. Why am I now so tired? It's mid-October, but I refuse to believe I am suffering from what is probably "just a cold." I consider the day before. In passing, I mention to an acquaintance whose mother lives in the Bronx that I am staying at a place off of the 4 train, near Kingsbridge Road. I assume he is as unfamiliar as I am with the area, but he catches me off guard. "Have you been to the park nearby? If not, go."

○

Narrative carries me like a wave and towards the holes.

○

It's through these holes that I take in the breath of the world. (Jeanne Hyvrard)

○

If the rush of not-knowing is also desire

○

5

A desire to ride off on an idealess horse

○

How shall I speak of my body
And its relationship to FORM?

○

My personhood, those boundaries, like sawdust

○

Dispersed (not unshaped, just undecided) and yet:

○

Upon walking through St. James Park, I noted a sudden internal rearranging of the parts. *But this is not at all cinematic,* I thought. Aside from the film, I had no memory of this place that was once a low marshland before it was graded with ash and soil, and then transformed into a park.

○

Now an accumulation of garbage, litter, and glass;

○

Or that which you cannot expel (these, the shards)

○

As if by sorting through it, I could finally say
"This" is why "that" happened
"This" is how "I" got here; that ligament, torn

○

It was not an address to which I wished to return

○

○

○

The day I first met H., I ordered over thirty dollars' worth of food at a nearby café. What I ate is unmemorable save for what I drank: a soda of rosemary, spruce, juniper, and sage. *Can I trust H. to help me, or am I too far gone?* I took another sip of my drink and thought of @On_Kawara.

I AM STILL ALIVE.

But feeling alive was causing me problems. The past few months, I had become increasingly disturbed by the idea that I did not deserve to live, not because I didn't want to try, but because I imagined I wasn't very good at it (to which H. would respond, "Say more about that").

I had never been a "happy" person. I had just *been*. And for whatever reason, just being felt inadequate. Then R. died; R. with whom I danced. R. with whom I once lived. He was the same R. who continued to seek me out even as I acted towards him somewhat distant and uncertain.

After R. died, away went my focus. I didn't lack the words so much as feel overwhelmed by their direction. Where were they carrying me, and what if I was not ready to follow? You are where your ghost lives. Sometimes living in two places at once (Minnesota and New York) caused me to feel as though I did not live anywhere because no one ever knew where I was.

As I finished my soda, I began to read on my iPhone an essay published earlier that morning by an author of notable repute. I held my breath and saw a stranger pass. *That violación. Que casi me destruyó.* Some people felt that to say so, in print, was an anticipatory gesture—a smoke screen for something worse. I thought of my friend A., the novelist. "And if it is?"

○

○

○

Why did I feel inside the wreckage that even if I was with you I was also so alone? At the corner of 193rd and Jerome, I worried as to whether or not it was at all possible to know myself outside of that photo of the young girl surrounded by concrete, brick, wire, and stone. "Because as you touch, you are being touched," reflected the choreographer Morgan Thorson in an interview about her latest collaborative dance work with sound artist Alan Sparhawk, titled *Public Love.*

(And if touch is a stand-in for something it is not?)

Back in Minneapolis, three billboards downtown feature an abstract cluster of hand, body, and garment, and in plain white text read the words PUBLIC LOVE. Somewhere between advertisement and public art, the gesture is reminiscent of Felix Gonzalez-Torres, who said to me in a dream the April before you died, "This is not about representation." It's not even about touch.

○

○

○

Give me a body I can in language throw

○

Around the waiting but before the alarm

○

○

○

"I've always wanted to have sex to music like this," E. says on our way to the holiday function.

"What?"

The day after we saw the opening-night performance of *Public Love*, I ordered a copy of Alan Sparhawk's 2006 album, *Solo Guitar*. I had been listening to it while I drove, usually alone, from home to therapy, and from therapy to work. It was moody, dark, wordless, apocalyptic, like Jim Jarmusch's *Only Lovers Left Alive* or Abel Ferrara's *4:44 Last Day on Earth*. *Had music ever figured prominently in my sex life?* I wondered. I remembered having sex once with M. to that song "Goodbye Horses," but that encounter was more fun-between-friends than it was hot.

"I just thought it would be, you know, interesting. To do it to something so . . . abstract."

I felt compelled by suggestion to imagine how interesting: E. in a room filled with bright, warm natural light, fucking; it would be so calm that all one would feel was not the sex, but the sound.

○

The number of high-priority
Emergency Medical Service
calls in the Bronx in 1988: 78.

○

There on the bed is a bouquet of roses;

They are neither an apology nor a gift.

○

○

○

From inside the wreckage emerged
a form.
It pressed its face against the wall—

○

○

○

Upon rewatching *Something Wild*, I hit PAUSE to consider the image of Mary Ann's cross (and the crisis of loss). How a violation can sever the soul from the body and make ruin where there was once a sense of belief, beauty. In an interview, the director, Jack Garfein, says his ambition is to depict through his film the experience of a person who has undergone a trauma. Unable to recall Garfein's exact words, I oscillate between verbs: *Undergone. Underwent. Suffered.* I am not confident in the ways I want to describe, or in the ways I try to remember. I hesitate over my desire to connect with others, particularly Mary Ann, a fictional character with actual feelings.

○

○

○

What if inside the pain is not a knowing you could hold

○

That which fails to coalesce (a form)

○

And the chalk that outlines the holes

○

○

○

What is the sound of paper burning

○

Or the sensation of energy moving—

○

As we become just the take of what leaves (Melissa Buzzeo)

○

A reaching towards the roaring

○

—a sudden rush of epinephrine:

○

A vision of the life you never had

○

And the knowledge that you are not dead

○

But by the time she came to, the moment was past.

○

In my dream was I not dragged?

○

YOU CAN LIVE LONG IT ISN'T PREDETERMINED (Hannah Weiner)

○

And yet afterwards I felt my essence wrought

○

The shadow beside two bodies that were one

○

A photo by Dawoud Bey, *Bronx*, 1981.

○

What if the only face of desire I recognize is loss?

○

○

○

Not only had I happened, but I was likely never to happen again.

That is how R. made me feel, like I was "the final girl"; i.e., Kirsty Cotton (*Hellraiser*, 1987), Nancy Thompson (*A Nightmare on Elm Street*, 1984), Sarah Connor (*The Terminator*, 1984).

○

I had seen so much violence, and yet I lived

○

To speak of the fracture that structures the telling

○

To exhume the past; to bury the present

○

Her mind was a circle of a few violent moments. (Alex Karmel)

○

○

○

I began to feel a persistent misalignment in my face.

Stop eating so many raw almonds. Sit up straight. Buy a bite guard. Meditate. When I tried to describe this sensation to others, I felt very inept. I used words like *broken* and *asymmetrical*. "But my jaw feels out of place," I complained. In the mirror, it appeared deviated, so on the recommendation of an acupuncturist, I made an appointment with S., who specializes in intraoral neuromuscular massage therapy. We met a few weeks later in an exam room at a clinic I sometimes visited. "Have you ever experienced a trauma?" she asked. It was such a direct question, I had to recalibrate. Did she mean specifically in regard to my face? "Like a car accident? No." She then stepped out so I could have a few moments alone to undress. I lay faceup on the heated table and pulled the sheet up as far as it would go. Naked from the waist up, I felt embarrassed and also tense. Her question gave me pause. Had something happened to me once? S. entered the room again. "Do you mind the music?" A binaural tone, then a swerve.

○

○

○

Note: the viscous pulsing along the pericardium

○

[. . .] rhythmic rather than the shape of your soul

○

Words arrived I did not know I knew

○

All memory. Occupies the entire. (Theresa Hak Kyung Cha)

○

But how without a form—?

○

If inside of the waves I am part of the pulsing

○

Safe: "in one piece"; alive and unharmed

○

○

○

Like cymbals, the touching was percussive.

○

I registered its movement, a bilateral progression.

○

"Why is this like drugs?" I could hardly hear myself speak, the words were so slurred.

Faceup, once again, I felt certain parts of me fall back, allowing others to reveal themselves. S. continued to work the muscles surrounding the temporomandibular joints in and around the mouth. It was as though, through touch, S. had activated some deep prehistoric reflex in my cells that, many lifetimes ago and in another form, may have once been employed via venom-producing-like glands whose presence I suspected based on the profound chemical changes they precipitated.

When I attempted to describe this experience to H., he said, "It sounds like you were relaxed." I laughed. "I guess?" But it was so much more dynamic than that. My body was like the meeting point between two screens made of mesh. The point at which they connect. It never felt like writing, and it never felt like sex, the sensation of the parts falling away and peeling back. It was as if I were immobilized by a spontaneous flood of snake blood, saliva, proteins, and polypeptides.

○

—is the secret we take away with us—touch (Susan Howe)

○

What if we are part of the black and blue—

○

The changing angle of the sun

○

Having failed to arrive
at a recognizable point
in space, lacking direction,
"I" was therefore lost.

○

○

○

On Monday, a snowstorm was expected to land, bringing with it
three to six inches of snow, subzero record lows, and hundreds of
school closures throughout northern and central Minnesota, so
H. emailed me to ask if I would prefer to cancel our upcoming ses-
sion or, alternatively, try to meet by phone. I was tempted to can-
cel because I wasn't at all sure how we would materialize in this
new circumstance; who would we be without our bodies? How
would we show up? I was made anxious by all the unknowns.
Then I felt guilty: I was aroused.

"Hello?"
"Hi! H—? It's me. Uh . . . How's it going?!"
I sounded way too eager.

"It's going . . ."

○

Between recounting my trip back to New York ("It was exhaust-
ing, it was cold, and I might as well have stayed home.") and a
dream about my extended family ("Someone should have apolo-
gized . . ."), a part of me felt like I was wilting; "Just to talk about it
makes me feel tense."

"Are you tense right now?"

We endured a long silence. I began to sweat. H.'s question ampli-
fied the source of my distress. It was a question about my body, the
fact that he was not there to see it. I wanted to hang up; the provo-
cation reminded me too much of phone sex (but how could he
have known that).

○

○

○

Felt the fracture widen;
the blue intervals, open

○

Not unlike my dream about the Bronx.

○

The cabdriver wanted to know where to drop me off, but I had no
answers, only a heightened awareness that I did not know, I did
not belong, and it would soon be dark.

○

So I ran towards the sex; I threw myself at the stars.

○

○

○

The figure of the urban wanderer (often male) is generally known as "the flâneur." According to Merlin Coverley's book *Psychogeography*: "Both [Charles] Baudelaire and [Walter] Benjamin locate the *flâneur*'s literary conception within a short story by Edgar Allan Poe ['The Man of the Crowd']." Poe once lived in the Bronx at 2640 Grand Concourse. You can still visit his house.

○

The act of cutting through from one place to another
produces a certain complexity
involving depth perception. (Gordon Matta-Clark)

○

In other words, inside the thrashing was us.

○

And although it was not garbage day
I thought: I have not been called
upon by the face of the person I loved

○

I stuttered at the thought

○

And abridged the text—

○

At the opposite end, on the studio floor, the cuts

○

And inside the pain, a wandering absence of place

○

I felt myself called to by the white noise of the shore

○

What if the nothing is not a place where one can live

○

If in the breakdown of the body there / Is nothing but smoke
(Melissa Buzzeo)

○

And if these are not my themes, is this still my narrative?

○

○

○

"I" is just a subject position. An orientation, a wandering

○

Whose expression is contingent upon the face it is facing;

○

In the behind-the-scenes-style documentary *Bronx Gothic*, which follows choreographer and performer Okwui Okpokwasili on the final tour of her solo performance of the same name, Okpokwasili reflects that the work's gothic elements revolve around "these hidden spaces, these doors that you best not open, the wings that you don't go into that hold . . . secrets, or spirits . . ."

○

In the moments before the mansion's collapse in Edgar Allan Poe's short story "The Fall of the House of Usher," a panic-ridden Usher confesses of his deceased twin sister, the lady Madeline, *"We have put her living in the tomb!* Said I not that my senses were acute?" When I asked H. why someone would want to bury a girl alive, he may have replied, "To bury the evidence."

○

Is this story too then in that tradition: the lineage
Of women who refused to stay hidden,
The lineage of bodies that refuse to stay buried

○

○

○

In Herb Goro's *The Block* (1970), an investigative photo-essay and anthropological study of one block in the East Bronx, everyone—from the sanitation worker to "the boy with the birds"—has an opinion about the growing garbage pit on the block, otherwise referred to as "the lot."

○

synonyms for *garbage: dross*
*refuse      debris      rot*

○

What more do you need
to know other than
I lived, that I was born?

○

[What the neighbors thought they heard]

○

Herman Melville is buried in the Bronx

○

I address
the noise—
        inside—
        is it writing

○

○

○

A lapse insinuates itself into language. (Michel de Certeau)

○

In search of a dead bolt, a grammar, a thought, a door—

○

What if all that's left of me are the holes?

○

○

○

And upon the lee, the morning after, I was thrown.

○

By un-doing a building there are many aspects of the social con-
dition against which I am gesturing: to open a state of enclo-
sure . . . (Gordon Matta-Clark)

○

Wherein I bear witness to the jargon &
ask: is it sex—the voice—is it violence

○

. . . that thing through which we know what violation is.
(Jennifer Doyle)

○

And from the violence, the shape of my soul, hewn

○

How can I reconcile all
the voices while bearing witness to the violence

○

How can I be without border? (Julia Kristeva)

○

The perimeter of which is feminine in form:

○

what refuses to house
the nothing; what
refuses to wash ashore

○

○

○

S. had this manner of bringing me to the edge of my pain so that
no matter what I had experienced the session before, I was still
able to return and continue in the work, even when certain sen-
sations were, upon the lightest palpation, unbearable. I was moti-
vated by curiosity more than anything: How would "I" change if
I allowed myself to turn towards the pain, rather than live in con-
stant aversion of it? What followed felt like the fulfillment of
some necessary spiritual obligation; by doing the work, I am
learning that in order to live, I have to learn how to transition
from one state to the next—how to become nerve gas, hemotoxin,
and snake again.

○

To be without clarity;
To write out of focus.

○

○

○

Near the end, I visited R. in the hospital. One minute I was in the wrong elevator, the next minute, the wrong floor. *What is he doing here?* When we had last spoken on the phone maybe a week or so earlier, the boundaries separating this word from that one began to erode, and several minutes would pass when I could not understand him because wherever this new astral-shaped tumor was, it was pressing upon a place of importance—thankfully, not the place where a person's intent lives, but near the body's willful expression of it. In other words, R. was still R., but as he spoke, the words were like a language made out of melted parts. Who do we have to be in each moment to be what the other wants when being one's self can never feel good enough?

○

○

○

*debris,* from *debriser*: to break apart

○

what the waves carried forth was us

○

Not an assortment of volcanic glass

O

called into being by the ocean's love

O

the changing angle of the sun

O

A film I would prefer not to watch

O

How hard was it for you to tell me that you knew you were dying while knowing that it would be a different kind of hard for me to listen? This is only one among many questions I wish I had been less afraid to ask. Nervous, I spoke to the nurse on call instead. "So, how do you all know each other," she wondered, and with your eyes you said, "We go way back." Everybody laughed because we had arrived at that strange point where we no longer needed words to understand.

All the same, there didn't seem to be anything else to do but talk, so I told her how we'd known each other for something like sixteen years, and that we had become friends after you asked me to prom because your date bailed on you last minute, and on and on. It felt good to talk about us (rather than myself), but I also felt alone and confused. Among the feelings I did not share that day: *Where are our friends? I thought I made it clear that if there was ever a time to show up . . .*

I realize now in hindsight that I might have been expecting too much; everyone processes grief in their own time, and at that moment, I really needed to talk to someone about what I was losing, and how I remembered you even though you were sitting right there with us. Plus, that nurse was such a gossip—"A nude model, *really* . . ." She indulged me as much as I indulged her.

Then I heard you begin to weep. "Sorry, I'm just emotional," you said.

"No, I'm sorry." I realized I had been talking about you already in the past tense.

○

○

○

That summer I saw a four-legged animal running like light

○

My soul overlooking the sea, perched on a bluff

○

Every time I try
to undo that demand (what I mean is writing).

○

—Easy: let yourself go, *regress*. (Roland Barthes)

○

What if this is garbage (but, also, what if it isn't)?

○

Are you anyone outside of a divination, a descent

○

Gordon Matta-Clark saw that inside the cut, after the cut: form

○

Anarchitecture: the ragged diagonals that constitute "the world"

○

I wanted to account for the nothing firsthand, without a source;

○

And in the moments between moments when I wedge myself between two opposing rock faces, I ask myself, "Is this us?" Is this narrative? Is this writing? Tell me: Is this love.

○

The sound of an iron spade striking the cement floor:

○

And inside my love, a torch; not the sirens we ignored

○

○

○

I watched the palm fronds as they lay, bent.

○

Weathered, they took on a new form.

○

Today, a barbell; tomorrow, a sword.

○

Where were the words by which I felt possessed? I held a dried-out bay leaf synonymous with your death as I remembered your body, the way it changed, and changed again.

○

○

○

The summer before you died, I saw Ivy Baldwin's *Keen [No.2]* at the Abrons Arts Center Playhouse Theater, and while you have been dead almost a year, and the space of grief is so long, it feels strange to admit that I have been thinking about this one particular dance work for longer than you have not been on this earth. How can I go back to before this time? (I imagine H. answers, "You can't.")

○

To keen is to cry in mourning or lamentation, to weep without words. The custom ritualizes a grief that is multiple, choral, and feminine in form. As someone who cries more often than she would like, and deeper than those around me know what to do with, I take comfort in the fact that keening is an Irish mourning tradition, rather than, or not exclusively, a symptom of an emotional or feminine-adjacent defect (childishness, hysteria, excess estrogen, and so on).

○

In *Keen [No. 2]*, a dance that comprises various solos, duets, and structured improvisations, the space of mourning is suffused with light, tantric and expansive. It is a beautiful tribute to Lawrence Cassella, Baldwin's longtime friend and dance-company member who died of HLH, a rare autoimmune disease, in 2015. When asked about the grief that accompanies the obvious shifts in her creative process, Baldwin recalls, "It was the only thing I could make anything about. . . . What if you don't replace this person? What if you live there and embrace that hole?"

○

What if inside the black and blue is us

○

The moment I saw the sea, not the land

○

Approaching structural collapse /
separating
the parts at the point of collapse    (Gordon Matta-Clark)

○

When I met up with Justin Jones in Minneapolis to talk about the score he wrote for *Keen [No.2]*, he described the collaboration with Baldwin as one guided by intuition and a shared interest in "digging through movement to find resonance." I consider that resonance alongside the sonic elements of the work, which range from the minimal to the otherworldly; the aural intensities, dilations, and sense of wonder that emerge alongside the choreography, and maybe even coproduce it, are part of the ritual of keening, rather than an amplification of it. In other words, the movement is part of the sound, and the sound, part of the movement, "its pulse," to use Jones's words. Together they form the language of the elegy, an ecstatic coursing through.

○

○

○

Every time I tried to write
about the present, the nothing—it kept interrupting.

○

stay in the nothing
this story — not even writing
(Danielle Collobert)

○

Despite my fear, it did not occur to me to yell.

○

What part of speech is ourselves?

○

*Again you consider the sumptuous wreckage of the present.*
(Lisa Robertson)

○

The vowels that could not speak what was lost.

○

In the thoroughly investigated epidemiological study *A Plague on Your Houses: How New York Was Burned Down and National Public Health Crumbled* (1998), authors Deborah and Rodrick Wallace chronicle the various ways that parts of the Bronx and Brooklyn were systemically ravaged as a result of disastrous city policies initiated as far back as the 1960s. They argue that following the construction of the Cross Bronx Expressway, first conceived by Robert Moses, the shortsighted city policy that was used to justify the withdrawal of essential city services from vulnerable neighborhoods led to the infamous fire epidemics of the 1970s and the subsequent public health catastrophes that would continue to plague the Bronx well through the 1980s and 1990s. The systemic cuts to vital city services, or "planned shrinkage" as it is otherwise known, limited citizens' access to adequate fire-control resources, functional public transportation, and reliable emergency health care. As a result, "what could burn did."

○

As buildings were abandoned, and neighborhoods destroyed, researchers like Deborah and Rodrick Wallace were able to corroborate that the instability precipitated by the new urban policy was accompanied by a noticeable increase in disorderly activities that included, but were not limited to, drunkenness, substance abuse, and compulsive promiscuity; these behaviors, combined with the added stresses that accompany poverty, the threat of arson, and a scarcity of safe, affordable housing, had in turn caused a surge in the number of crimes such as vandalism, robbery, and death by homicide. The incidences of HIV, measles, and tuberculosis rose during this time as well. In the words of Deborah and Rodrick Wallace, "Disasters to which responses are inadequate or inappropriate ripple out and amplify, engendering further disaster."

31

O

My sense of time, even my sense of touch
is shaped by the death I write towards now

O

What can you tell me about biofluorescence?

O

Those bodies that emit light but

O

(Only under certain conditions)

O

Single-celled, could I but touch

O

The face of the person I recognized out of love

O

And if the mastodons in the dream are also me?

O

As if on the verge of a threshole—hold

O

I approach the point of
entry,
the moment just before


○


It can take light-years for me to land on a word


○


In one of his early "building cut" projects *Bronx Floors* (1972–73),
artist and "anarchitect" Gordon Matta-Clark entered condemned
and abandoned buildings in the Bronx and elsewhere and cut out
sections of the interiors, walls, and floors. Matta-Clark would
then photograph the cuts from vantage points that rearranged the
optics of space; you could be staring at either a hole in the ceiling
or, depending on your perspective, a hole in the floor. One of the
works from this series, a diptych titled *Threshole,* exhibits a cut
that was made beneath a door between what one imagines were
once two separate rooms. Even though it's not my favorite from
this series, I feel a gravitational pull towards the concept which,
through wordplay, captures Matta-Clark's ambition "to trans-
form place into a state of mind by opening walls where doors
never were."


○


The artist had managed to graft a poetic idea onto a space while
curiously maintaining an approach that strikes me by today's
standards as pretty masculine in its relation to and understanding
of material, matter, form. As a woman writing alongside this work
(and maybe in homage), I have wondered how to translate that
process, a series of gestures, back into words.

○

Now go ahead and tilt your head back

○

:: Imagine the line as a load-bearing wall ::

○

○

○

Why is Herman Melville buried in the Bronx?

○

At such a crossing, halt—

○

○

○

In April, E. and I attended a 35 mm screening of *1990: The Bronx Warriors* (1982), directed by Enzo G. Castellari. According to the program, the film was "shot on the mean streets of early 1980s New York City, with gang members as part of the cast." It also boasts, "Castellari's super fun exploitation flick gets better with every year." Alongside films like *Wolfen* (1981) and *Tenement* (also known as *Slaughter in the South Bronx*, 1985), *The Bronx Warriors*, as well as its sequel, *Escape from the Bronx* (1983), is part of the short-lived subgenre known as Bronxploitation, whose imagery derives from a paranoid assortment of 1970s news-media-touted clichés that both sensationalized and profited from the Bronx's record number of abandoned and burned out buildings, its reputation as an arson-ridden, crime-infested wasteland, and the unsubstantiated belief that were it not for those uncivilized and uneducated Blacks and Puerto Ricans (and their guns, gangs, and graffiti), New York City would not have gone to complete shit.

○

DESTROY ALL LINES. (Skeme, *Style Wars,* 1983)

○

Followed by a stress-induced gesture marked
by the spasming of the bronchi inside the lungs

○

NO BODY
NO FORM

○

With all of the odds against them, the inner city youths of the 1970s managed to create "something" that they could claim as their own. They called it "writing." (Phase 2)

○

We live with the uncertainty of not knowing when

○

The middle of the story keeps asking to become the end
(Daniel Borzutzky)

○

Richard Serra's first major outdoor exhibition, *To Encircle Base Plate Hexagram, Right Angles Inverted* (1970), was located at 183rd Street and Webster Avenue in the Bronx. The artist's sculpture was included in the Whitney Annual, though he complained no one went to go see it.

○

what is a language
that refuses to be
read; a sentence
that refuses to end:

○

"The place in the Bronx was sinister, used by local criminals to torch the cars they'd stolen. There was no audience for the sculpture in the Bronx, and it was my misconception that the so-called art audience would seek the work out." —Richard Serra, 1980

○

I was there and yet I have no memory of that performance.

○

"[There] is a type of space we all . . . have stored in memory: spaces that are detailed and precise, fragments generally, at all levels of reminiscence. And, of course, once you get into reminiscence, an infinite number of associations emerge." —Gordon Matta-Clark

○

the enigmatic bits of drift (Valéry)

○

What can barely contain the nothing—

○

a black out
a threshole
a time jump                    a cut

○

A cut that took three days and six inches of rain.
(Gordon Matta-Clark)

○

How old were you
when you learned
to negate a thing? I . . .

Be more specific: I.

○

It is the body that must transform itself into writing.
(Michel de Certeau)

○

Because of the ways that text had, in a previous life, been
disparaged.

○

In November 1980, Sophie Calle's *The Bronx* was first exhibited at the South Bronx–based alternative arts space Fashion Moda, located at 2803 Third Avenue. The work, which was initially titled *Waiting for People to Come to Fashion Moda and Asking Them to Take Me Wherever They Want in the South Bronx,* was part of a citywide group exhibition, *Une Idée en l'Air.* In Calle's words: "I was the 'afterthought' so . . . I inevitably got the Bronx." Whereas it would have been a bigger break to show one's work downtown, Calle was not discouraged; it was her first public exhibition. From Thursday, November 6, to Friday, November 14, the artist invited random passersby whom she met at Fashion Moda to take her wherever they wanted—"a place that they'd never forget." Among the sites to which she was brought: Yankee Stadium, the Botanical Garden, a rubble-filled lot on Morris Avenue blessed by the pope. Calle documented her experiences through a combination of photograph, interview, and text, and in this way, the resulting work appears fairly straightforward: a portrait of the Bronx. The night before the show's opening, after the artist had installed the work, "an unexpected and providential collaborator broke into the gallery and covered every possible surface with graffiti." Looking back on *The Bronx* some years later, Calle concluded the final result was "much better."

○

Inside the closeness was not a knowing we could hold

○

committed to the Nothing-in-between— (John Cage)

○

what became of you, your soul
after your body washed ashore

○

bone, reef, scale, stone

○

I searched for you, you whom I could never know

○

Inside the roaring, the white noise of the shore

○

The hesitation you hold in your throat

○

From May 16 to June 30, 1992, the Museum of Modern Art exhib-
ited Felix Gonzalez-Torres's *"Untitled" (Billboard),* an enlarged
photographic image of the artist's empty, unmade bed. Measuring
in at 10'5" tall and 22'8" wide, the image was displayed on twenty-
four billboards at various sites across New York City, as well as in
the museum. If you are familiar with the work of Felix Gonzalez-
Torres, then maybe you know why twenty-four; see, for example,
*"Untitled" (Last Light)* (1993) or *"Untitled" (Perfect Lovers)* (1991).

○

While most of the empty-bed billboards were on view throughout
parts of Manhattan, two of them were located in the Bronx—one
at 144th Street and Grand Concourse, the other at 2511 Third
Avenue and East 137th Street.

○

At what point do these histories collapse

○

And what words can "I"
ascribe to the fracture that structures the telling

○

The knowledge that what we miscarried was us

○

I followed you into the nothing, like a wave, and then was

○

From the Museum of Modern Art's press release for the show:
"These billboards will remain in place only through the end of
June [5/16/92–6/30/92]. Twenty-four in number, they commemo-
rate the date of the death of the artist's lover, Ross. At the end of
June, they too shall pass, torn down to make way for new images,
new messages, new meanings."

○

How do you come back from
that
for which there are no words

○

Nor means of return;

○

There isn't a day I don't ask myself, "Is this the day
I want to go to that place," the wreckage I call home

○

My feet, at night, carried by the glow

○

A list of sixteen verbs (in the style of Richard Serra's *Verb List*):

| | | | |
|---|---|---|---|
| to excavate | to stress | to burn | to tear |
| to exhume | to break | to ruin | to shake |
| to unearth | to cut | to leave | to lose |
| to disinter | to cave | to trace | to wake |

○

○

○

In the film *The Taking of Pelham One Two Three* (1974), four men,
Mr. Blue, Mr. Green, Mr. Grey, and Mr. Brown, board a Brooklyn-
bound 6 train with the intent of hijacking it for a million dollars'
ransom. The train leaves the Pelham Bay Park Station in the Bronx
at 1:23 p.m.

○

According to IMDB: "Since the film's release, no #6 train has ever
been scheduled to leave Pelham Bay Park Station at either 13:23 or
01:23 by the New York City Transit Authority."

○

Ensconced within: a revelation about my practice

○

Is that superstitious, to speak of a fateful collision

○

The time between movements; the caesura, the hold

○

What happened to you in the interim (had I known)

○

I saw my soul on the tracks illuminated by the glow

○

I lay down with the nothing

○

(What you can't keep, burn)

○

What is the animal inside this feeling

○

Slurring over, I had all but belonged

○

Once, I too lived off the 6

○

In a blue taffeta gown, I wrote the words

○

○

○

On my way back to Minneapolis, seated next to me on the plane is V., a drug counselor from Queens who looks a little like Pam Grier. When she asks me where I'm from, I say, "I was born in the Bronx," and she is all about it, cheering, "There you go—I knew she had it going on!"

As V. pulls out her Galaxy S8 Plus and asks me to cozy up to her so we can take a selfie midflight, I notice her fresh baby-blue acrylic tips, and flash back to Nomi Malone, played by Elizabeth Berkley (also known as Jessie from *Saved by the Bell*) in the nineties classic *Showgirls,* directed by Paul Verhoeven. Nomi, an aspiring topless dancer who dreams of making it big as the premier showgirl in *Goddess* at the Stardust Casino, is volatile, childish, unstable, and, my favorite, X-RATED. She reacts to everything in excess; she's over the top. From the way she dances (like she's "fucking") to the way she ketchups her french fries, it is all too much.

In the context of the film, that wildness, which typically expresses itself as a gendered inability to manage the exhilarating manic highs and lows of it all, is what gives Nomi her edge; why bother keeping it together? It's fucking Las Vegas; you either go there to win or not at all.

But I was nowhere near Las Vegas. I was thirty-five hundred feet above sea level.

○

○

○

These formless, blue half-truths
We would prefer to hide inside;

○

What if you're the most perceptive person I know?

○

Knowing: not as recitation but as / The unhinging somatic event
(Forrest Gander)

○

Whose beauty I begin to approach

○

Whose love against which I brace myself

○

A resident of 601 Pelham Parkway North and member of the Art Deco Society of New York said, "I want to restore the building and make it as beautiful as it was in 1937, when it opened."

○

To open a state of enclosure

○

To disappear the restoration

○

To be as beautiful as you once were

○

To come into contact
with that which
you cannot hold

○

The South Bronx is home to the second-largest number of art moderne and art deco buildings in the United States. First is Miami Beach. Art moderne is more streamlined than art deco.

○

And, inside the curves, also love.

○

The point at which they intersect

○

Not every collision is an accident

○

If I speak from a subject position that is no longer

○

I carry the weight of the body that moves forward

○

How do you come back from that for which there are no words?

○

Between an opening and an impasse

○

Had I recognized the sea, not the land

○

And that before your death, first, went

○

The words

○

While you lived and yet—

○

I lost sight of the shore

○

By the mid-1970s, the deteriorating conditions of the South Bronx
started to spread to parts of the West Bronx, including the once
majestic Grand Concourse, home to so much Bronx deco.

○

I thought of my country's body

○

Not the shape, but the shores

○

Between being and nonbeing;

○

Was.

○

But duration or continuity can also be achieved
by a very careful and dexterous manipulation of interruptions.
(Maya Deren, "Creative Cutting")

○

Imagine saying so not out loud.

○

From where, and with what force?

○

The specter of this, my death

○

That which I stutter to address

○

With no route to write myself

○

Forward, rather than "home"

○

If this leads me nowhere, close
to the nothing, where shall I go

○

○

○

On the phone I speak with A., whom I met years ago in New York
but who now lives in Vermont, somewhere remote. She tells me
about her house and her new cat, Gloria, and a party on July 4. We
also speculate about perception, how we discover a person, their
mannerisms, and come to know what governs them.

We are not talking about actual people. A. is a novelist, so we're
really talking about characters, which are knowable in ways that
real people are not. She asks me if I've ever considered the pos-

sibility that a person acts the way they do because they have experienced at a young age "a knowledge-producing event." I laugh because it is very A. of her to ask this kind of question.

"That's elegant," I say. "No, it's never occurred to me to describe a knowledge-producing event as anything other than a trauma."

In the space between question and answer, I wondered what series of knowledge-producing events might have structured my friend's query, so unique and considerate of the unknowable experiences of others. It's O.K. not to know everything. I conclude that the nature of our friendship is such that were I ever to inquire about these events, the confirmation of their having happened would never be as interesting as the person I may or may not know as A.

○

○

○

The open suitcase—is it a coffin or a boat?

○

A presence you cannot disclose erodes

○

The violent movement, a turning towards

○

What holes, and made of what? (Anne Carson)

○

I wrote my breath inside a surge in reverse

O

And recalled your essence, through glass, thrown

O

When you looked at me, what was it that you saw?

O

the severed surface which reveals
the autobiographical process of its making. (Gordon Matta-Clark)

O

My shape refracted through the violence

O

From inside the serrated edge scribbled

the words *you*

*must, you can, inconsequentially, again*

O

O

O

In Cassavetes's *Gloria* (1980), Gena Rowlands's character lives in
the Concourse Plaza Hotel at 900 Grand Concourse. Other nota-
ble Bronx landmarks that make a cameo in the film include
Yankee Stadium and the Bronx Museum of the Arts.

○

Among those highly stylized ruins, I felt my legs go numb. *Walk it off*, I thought. I ended up at an exhibition of the painter Mary Weatherford the day before it closed. Initially, after a few minutes in the gallery, I felt disappointed. The paintings were large, formally interesting, and abstract. At their most beautiful, they reminded me of graffiti: irresponsible and committed. Unexpected. And yet for the most part, these paintings, despite the fact that they were illuminated by their neon parts, did not emanate light. Not from within, anyway. Except for one, *GLORIA*. It was soft, haphazard, glowing. I immediately recalled 1980 Gena Rowlands, the various mauves, pinks, and satins she wears throughout the film. A beautiful character study, I thought, and left the show satisfied. I later confirmed that it was actually the painting *next* to this painting that was *GLORIA;* the one I so admired was *Soft Pink Copper Eagle.*

○

In the wake of the burnout we stood
under a ceiling lined with leaflets of gold foil.

○

How do you represent that which is not known

○

When trauma renders the lyric episodic;

○

My essence, shorn.

○

And in excess, known.

○

I followed you into the nothing, and then, was.

○

You appeared at the edge of a still life

while I waited

for the words

○

And in the looking, saw us

○

And in the breaking, love;

○

And in the holes, us. And in the cuts, us.

○

I held the breaking and called it love

○

I threw the brick and called it thought

○

Why did we think we could breathe with one lung

○

(NO TRESPASSING) the sign read

○

Thus, into the world, my soul was sent—

○

Like a wave
that carries the garbage
leeward upon the shore

○

And whispered the words, "Never again."

○

○

○

What if this poem is a poem about the end

○

A violent succession of several perforations

○

The surface from which I withdraw my hand

○

For *Untitled (Bricks)* (1982–83), Tim Rollins, who has described himself as "a Conceptual artist whose medium is teaching," assigned students of I.S. 52 in the South Bronx with the task of scouring an abandoned lot across the street in search of some object that they could reclaim as their own. One of the children found a brick, and upon returning to the classroom, decided to paint it as though it were a building on fire. It must have been a real moment for Rollins that day because he gathered the rest of the students and returned to the lot; more bricks were collected, painted, and transformed into little burning tenements. They then sold their bricks for five dollars apiece at the A. More Store, a pop-up artist shop run by the artist collective Colab. In 1984, some of the bricks were exhibited at Fashion Moda (although I wouldn't see them for the first time until years later as part of the show *Macho Man: Tell It to My Heart,* curated by Julie Ault).

○

Rollins was barely twenty-six when he started teaching in the Bronx and began the Art and Knowledge Workshop, or what would later become K.O.S. These bricks, which, to use the words of one critic, were "salvaged from ubiquitous rubble that littered their neighborhood and painted to look like the flaming buildings from which they had come," were K.O.S.'s first publicly exhibited sculpture. Therefore, K.O.S. was born in the Bronx. While K.O.S. stands for *Kids of Survival,* apparently one of the kids identified with the moniker because it sounded kind of like CHAOS.

○

(In my notes after having seen the documentary:
*Puerto Ricans + Schubert = Radical Pedagogy*)

○

In *Housing in New York: A Brief History, 1960–2007,* the artist
Glenn Ligon describes the public housing apartment complex in
which he lived from 1960 to 1973 as "a Le Corbusier fantasy
transplanted to the South Bronx." Among my favorites of Ligon's
works (and there are many) are some seventeen enlarged archival
prints of the artist's studio copy of James Baldwin's 1953 essay
"Stranger in the Village." An accumulation of fingerprint, margi-
nalia, splatter, and smudge, the series, titled *What We Said The
Last Time,* constitutes something of a reader's diary, and this text
was *read.* While the prints are beautiful and unmistakably Glenn,
what I am drawn to in them above everything else is the style of
reading they embody, an American optimism inherited from
Baldwin, I'd guess, that believes in the rigorous, unpredictable
sanctity of study.

○

○

○

In 1966, snow leopards arrived at the Bronx Zoo.

○

"It was too much to *take in* photographically."
Frank Gimpaya, *Images from the South Bronx*

○

What if there's nothing? What if there's not.

○

So that when I say "I," I am in fact invoking us

○

A series of sequins, like bacteria, but pelagic

○

So that when the shoal swerved we went with it

○

Because we are energy as well its displacement

○

We who were redirected

○

And we who made the most of it

○

Sometimes I felt not the force, but its pull

○

I move forward but not of my own accord

○

○

○

In December 1989, Sophie Rivera installed six 45-by-36-inch black-and-white photographs at Yankee Stadium and 161st Street. The series was titled *Revelations: A Latino Portfolio.*

In one portrait, a man with a mustache wears a coat with a flashy fur-lined hood; his eyebrows, equally voluminous, blend in with the ostentatious curve of his cowl.

In another, a man with a beauty mark faces the photographer; he appears somber and unguarded. Like the others, he is *Untitled,* anonymous. "Incandescent." Rivera chose her subjects by asking passersby outside her apartment building in the Bronx if they were Puerto Rican; those who answered yes were invited to pose for her in her studio against a wood-paneled backdrop. She produced at least fifty of these silver gelatin portraits, but only fourteen survived a studio fire.

○

○

○

The kind of portrait one could resurrect

○

Not on the telephone. Slurring the words.

○

I had all but belonged.

○

Speechless; mottled.

○

& thus, transformed;

○

When R. died, I couldn't chase after the thing I had been anymore.

○

I could not trust that there was a silver
chain waiting for me inside of the gold

○

Real freedom, as an act of perception, has no form.
(Clarice Lispector)

○

○

○

And then we rotated in the blue light of April

○

The knowing, its sex, without a body, circulates

○

It accumulated like snow, and it wasn't personal

○

I saw your living as necessary and unpredictable, though it wrote
me letters. It drove me home.

○

Even if there was nothing, we would still have us.

○

I know because, by the feminine grace of God, whenever I move my hands, there you are.

○

○

○

After visiting OSMOS at 50 East 1st Street to view some works by Bronx-born painter and photographer Darrel Ellis, I consider the work that memory does, the way it makes itself known and, in response to feeling, changes, transforms. How does a person integrate loss? I recall a line from Etel Adnan: "One can't think without remembering." That truth is inscribed in so much of Darrel's work; the absence that materializes in his art, particularly the works that reinterpret his father's idyllic black-and-white family photographs, often refers back to a closeness that never was. In 1958, Darrel's father, Thomas, a postal clerk and aspiring photographer who briefly ran a portrait studio in Harlem with his wife, was murdered at age thirty-three after the injuries sustained from an argument with two plainclothes police detectives over Thomas's blocked parked car proved fatal. The incident took place just months before Darrel was born. Justice was never served.

○

In an interview, Darrel observes of his father's negatives and his own repeated referencing of them throughout his process: "When I look at those photographs sometimes, all I see is holes."

○

I wrote. I stretched. I let language in

○

Yes, that's graffiti; no, that's language

○

So sharp so bright so brittle so broken

○

○

○

There has to be something
in this marathon of feeling

○

(I wanted to believe that what I held was a diamond)

○

a carbon-based life-form
Something worth saving

○

So that the rest of the world could remain imperfect

○

○

○

In *You Do the Crime, You Do the Time* (1976), a two-part filmic
portrait of the South Bronx street gang the Roman Kings, cinema-

tographer Martine Barrat interviews sixteen-year-old Vickie, then president of the Roman Queens. The two smoke cigarettes while discussing Vickie's writing, her experiences growing up in the Bronx, and the murder of her close friend Edna by a rival gang. Vickie speaks candidly with Barrat about the display coffin Edna was buried in and the way she and her friends defaced it; for had they not found a way to claim this coffin as their own, it would have been promptly returned to the funeral parlor following the service, leaving Edna interred in a pine box. I respect that kind of loyalty, born out of love. The conversation continues, but my attention drifts, now distracted by the threat of the pine box.

When Barrat shared a longer cut of the film at the Whitney in 1978—the featured footage, over one hundred hours' worth—she explained, "I saw the violence in the conditions and not in the children."

○

○

○

What is essence? A hole or a body? (Antonin Artaud)

○

That split, it radiated along a longitudinal axis

○

Always a cold sore, never a rogue horse

○

It may not be obvious, but it is inelegant

○

Undone by love, I had no choice but to open

○

The double doors that lead to the right atrium

○

And the beautiful green of the botanic garden

○

Beautiful green possibilities without interruption

○

○

○

Here, there. Minneapolis, the Bronx. Inside my thought is always a second thought, an afterwards to where I originally was. In this way, a parenthetical helps me occupy

two places at once
(two times at once)

○

The time of the sentence and the time after

○

(Am I guilty now of being post-nostalgic?)

○

Parentheses allow me to retreat from myself, as well as to say something else. For whom are such secret missives intended? Whoever is listening, I guess. When I'm writing, opposite me, there are always at least two people: somebody (an abstraction) sitting next to your ghost.

○

Parentheses outline the places you aren't.

○

. . . A strange malamute who goes by the name of "Mr. Shy Guy" (though he is 64.5 centimeters tall) scatters his hugeness when approached.

○

○

○

Inside me lead, arsenic ions floating

○

Rigorous grammatical investigations

○

I lick the brine that clouds my looking

○

○

○

Trampled, it forces you to find itself

○

Around the abattoir near the absence

○

Near the nonsense beyond the grasses

○

What if you felt split, but inside

○

Not split but with and inside the parts

○

○

○

Write the form you wish
to touch
then tend to it with rosin

○

○

○

When I ask S. during a session what drew her to the work, she replies, "The layers." Body as geological record: strata, rock, action. These, the shards. Tissue lets you discover it, and when it can, it gives way, yielding new impressions. In orienting my attention towards my body, its histories as well as its cellular capacities, S. is teaching me how to reconsider my own formlessness, the ways my person has been bound, unleashed, divided, and reborn. What it knows is older than I am; what it holds and gives of itself is more than I could ever recount.

○

Within that longing there was a blue light
coming at me from everywhere all at once

○

The beauty is that you can begin again

○

Open the inside of a clock. Now watch—

○

What I hold moves me so that I am breathless

○

Agitating
the fibers where the smooth muscle contracted

○

These are the sensations I wanted to chase. They are not always recognizable to me, the forms they take, or what, if anything, is meaningful about their particular expression apart from the fact that our acknowledgment of them—through touch—often leaves me mangled and estranged.

○

○

○

Arrest: A stop. A pattern in speech that cuts off thought;

○

You want to wave but it's not a gesture that makes sense.

○

I want to stop carrying the burdens that least define us.

○

There was something beautiful in that, the dissolution that we let in

○

The undoing chord, without port or object.

○

I swerved into the agrammatical (and then had sex)

○

Not every mistake should be erased. Nor shall the unintelligible be left out. (C. D. Wright)

○

○

○

Is this an elegy or a love song

○

rather than a story about the turnstiles

○

and the manner in which we jumped them

○

Should I be ashamed to wish myself dead
to want
my body to visit you wherever your body is

○

If only our past obsessions could
explain our current predicaments

○

○

○

Today I spoke to S. not of the eagles, but of experience.

○

How can one speak of the present when one feels abandoned by it?

○

A paragraph is a time and place, not a syntactic unit. (Lyn Hejinian)

○

I said what I needed was not love, but permission.

○

Carrot, cashew, turmeric;

○

In memory, it transforms.

○

We had arrived at the right street, wrong address.

○

Consciousness floated away. I could not catch up.

○

That's what makes it narrative.

○

It's not that I was breathed into. It was that *I lived*.

○

What we once were, I should never have devalued it.

○

○

○

When does one acquire a language?

○

Is it through repetition, bombardment, or experience?

○

*Whether or not* introduces a condition and its opposite.

○

When I think of the Bronx, I think of language coming
apart, always before me, threshing;
             Undone.

○

Insofar as I was aimless, "I" was
stranded between two sentences.

○

It was as if I had been scored somewhere below the surface

○

And subject to the order in which things reveal themselves;

○

Despite the style of their movements, their English a chorus.

○

"Let the energy do its work." I am trying to listen

○

To a particular kind of music to confirm that I am.

○

And then we exchanged particles. Electrons leapt.

○

Deconstructing the present is and is not an addiction.

○

Without enough sun, the leaves on the lime tree curl.

○

We don't have to come back. We don't have to know who we are.

○

We don't have to see ourselves reflected in the orb.

○

And if I cannot inhabit an idealess world?

○

I can absent myself from the weblike forms;

○

○

○

After I returned, I saw the plants had grown

○

When I say I had this sensation of S. welding the parts, I am try-
ing to communicate that in me, and in us, something was becom-
ing fused where it had once been torn. When heat was applied
along the body's fault lines, plates that were broken began to
realign and the beautiful blueness of the world broke through.
And S. would remark, "We went somewhere we never went before."

○

In my arms, the amplification.

○

The fossil self. Its derivatives.

○

To have delivered to you in person that tiger balm.

○

Months had passed. I could think of nothing but love.

○

Months had passed. I could think of nothing but loss.

○

Everything we need to live we carry inside; everything
we need is already in us to write.

○

So I saw my cruelty as if from the outside, and thought of the photographer Dora Maar.

○

But remember—whatever the technique, it must serve the form as a whole (Maya Deren)

○

○

○

Let your mind break long enough for THE NOTHING to take hold.

○

And if my life is undone by my own animal hand . . . ?

○

Any pit is an abyss, if properly labeled. (Susan Sontag)

○

○

○

I wanted to know what other people knew, and I really felt at age twenty-three, the same age that Clarice Lispector was when she started writing her second novel, *The Chandelier,* that I knew nothing. How to cut up a whole chicken, where to buy earplugs. The city in which my mother was born. Nothing.

○

Of Clarice Lispector, the poet Elizabeth Bishop, who once tried her hand at translating a few of Lispector's short stories, wrote her friend and literary confidante, Robert Lowell, to say, "She's the most non-literary writer I've ever known." In spite of my own literary training, I prefer the "non-literary" aspects of Lispector while also feeling hard-pressed to say exactly what these are.

○

to live in the time of the characters
rather than the time of the world—

○

In a class taught by choreographer and performer luciana achugar, which lasted for five days and encouraged participants to experience "being in pleasure" by "becoming uncivilized," I became acquainted with the following concepts:

Connecting with the fascia

Becoming a skin-body (e.g., a unicellular organism)

Seeing without knowing

These ideas, I gathered, are intentionally vague so as not to impose or suggest too strongly how one should become, be, or see. Unlike some of the other dancers in class, I had never seen luciana perform, so I had no frame of reference for how she applied these concepts, but I kept showing up because I felt encouraged by the possibility that such a practice might, as the class description suggested, allow one to experience "growing a new body; a connected body; an anarchic body; a utopian body . . ."

And so on the third day of class, as we practiced seeing without knowing, when I looked out the studio window and saw a damp, blue construction tarp flapping in the wind, I saw, through the skin underneath my eyes, not the tarp, but the makeshift roofs of the people in Puerto Rico.

○

The practice of being in pleasure is a political practice. When we allow ourselves to embrace pleasure by resisting conventional ideals of beauty, form, mastery, and intellect, we are also making room for something "instinctual, intuitive, improvisatorial," to use luciana's words.

Something connected.

○

○

○

We can reshuffle the cards—we can begin again.

○

What will you do with all that Himalayan sea salt

○

In memory of that knowing whose presence was.

○

A uniform glossy green; cells dying and dividing

○

The shards catch light on the cut, the edges give off sparks.
(Rosmarie Waldrop)

○

Now let your body drop

○

Do you recognize the face of the girl
who once played the harp?
Yes, she had one blue eye, one brown.

○

The girl on the train, her eyebrows an arc

○

"If you're listening." And tonight I was.

○

○

○

Layers of deep peach and dandelion disperse among the pumpkin
patch of poppy reds.

○

To myself I would like to bind them.

○

In the paintings of Ronnie Landfield, light comes from elsewhere. It just pours in, at the right moment, always at the golden hour, the magic hour, which either follows a sunrise or precedes a sunset. During the golden hour, daylight enters and gathers the day's various dreamy reds.

○

The Bronx is no longer a place I know, and yet I struggle still to recognize it.

○

○

○

"Those circles, are they an open mouth or a throat?"

○

wut is a hole if not a thynge 2 emptie (Jos Charles)

○

A circle without a center; A circle without content

○

To the photographer at the corner of Ryer and 184th

○

○

○

I woke up a little after 4 a.m. frustrated by the sensation in my left arm. It wasn't asleep exactly—that feeling was familiar enough—but it did feel less available, less present than the other parts. *What is happening to me?* It was as if I were a snake and I had two skins. My old skin was stretching to make room for the new one, and as the new one grew, learned to flex and take shape, it rubbed up against the dead tissue, the slough (also known as "the exuviae"). Scientists call this process "ecdysis." It can take anywhere from seven to fourteen days. *Never handle a snake that shows signs of an impending shed or is actively shedding,* the internet warns. First, I was filled with dread ("I'm dying"). Then, paranoia: When are metaphors useful, and when are they not? Maybe I had not taken enough B12, or maybe I had overzealously taken too much, and what I was experiencing was not some deep metaphysical change, but actually nerve damage. Or were these one and the same? Then I recalled something choreographer Michelle Boulé had said to me once: "We can't predict what forms healing will take." I rubbed my forearm, afraid of this process, its waywardness.

○

lacking the language-producing
parts of your body, your brain—

○

*Are you going to be the snake
or are you going to be the snake's cast-off skin?*
(Anne Boyer)

○

○

○

"So, you know how reality works, right?"

*Oh, fuck. What have I gotten myself into.*

It was Ash Wednesday when I decided to visit C., an energy healer who came recommended by way of S. What is suggested by the term "energy healer" is unclear to me. Maybe C. practiced Reiki, I have no idea, and yet to indulge my skepticism by inquiring more felt disrespectful. It was I who reached out to C., after all, and while I like to think of myself as an "empirical" kind of person, it would also be an exaggeration for me to claim that I had no expectations whatsoever of this kind of medicine, despite any reservations. I wanted the energy healing to work, and maybe for it to do so, I needed to be energetically open to the idea that it might, that it could . . .

"So, you know how reality works, right?"

I took a few moments to imagine the various ways one might respond: *Yes, yes, I know how reality works, so no need for the preamble!* Or: *No, I don't know. Please, tell me more.* Or maybe I would answer a question with a question: *Well, how do you know how reality works?*

"No one teaches us how to perceive formlessness."

I nodded, and relaxed into my chair. "That sounds about right . . ." And we took it from there.

However, I wasn't convinced that it was for me to learn how reality works, because I'm not convinced reality is a phenomenon one can "know," let alone summarize. C. seemed so sure of herself though, and I wanted desperately to believe. I did not feel compelled (again, out of respect) to initiate a debate, so I let her explain to me the fact of my "earth suit" (the body given to me by my parents) as it existed in "the external world," which she likened to the weather.

But rather than listen too intently, I instead recalled various scenes from George Kuchar's *Weather Diaries*. In his 1986–90 five-part series of weather dispatches from Oklahoma, Kuchar documents not just the weather, but his run-ins with motel neighbors, his eating habits, bowel movements, and what's on TV. Weather imagery is interspersed with an assortment of clips of local weather reports and special tornado programs, as well as shots of the motel interiors, notably, the toilet; these are presented in a somewhat haphazard manner alongside views of the sky, trees, and storm damage as seen from Kuchar's motel window.

Much of the footage is uneventful: fields, clouds, and TV commentary; and yet the dread associated with tornado season, power outages, hail, flash floods, and other freakish weather phenomena, are always looming. Kuchar dramatizes that dread, playing up his queer-outsider-Bronx-boy neuroses. The beautiful thing is: once you hear his voice, which is featured throughout *Weather Diaries* (and perhaps, most memorably, in the classic short "Hold Me While I'm Naked," which made its debut in 1966, twenty years earlier), you can never unhear it.

○

About *Weather Diaries,* Kuchar reflects, "This whole thing started because of my interest in nature. Since I was a city boy, living in the Bronx, nature came to me via the colorful tapestry of sky that loomed above the tenements. The awe of summer thunderstorms, smothering blizzards, and window rattling nor'easters left a lasting impression on me."

○

Without pattern, speechless

○

The circle sweats and expands

○

Allowing breath though resonant

○

And when it widens, it vibrates

○

In the space of écriture feminine

○

Another orifice through which the present insists

○

NO interiority without dimension;
NO interiority without perspective

○

Had I been born oriented towards it

○

Unstructured by my own repetitions

○

Disc-like though placeless—

○

Beyond narrative

○

Without entrance

○

○

○

The temporary experience of feeling cognitively rearranged was not always terrible. Sometimes, rather than ask S. too many questions, I would silently observe and appreciate the ways my suffering would change, particularly the moments when I didn't feel numb so much as disinterested in my own pain, the drama that it wrought. Could I be this accepting always?

○

So I threw myself
My whole person
With all my being

○

Towards a form that was always arriving

○

A shape so unlike my own, its essence

○

like light, refracted, the part of the waves

○

that were not part of this world—holographic

○

and thus languageless, I depart, and enter

○

what I sensed was experience: a violation

○

A red dog leaping without a sex to hold it

○

○

○

Steve McQueen's feature *Shame,* starring Michael Fassbender opposite Carey Mulligan, is often described as a portrait of a man struggling with sex addiction, though I have never been entirely convinced: It's not that the film *isn't* about that—McQueen describes in countless interviews following the film's release that in order to write the screenplay, he and his coauthor, Abi Morgan, traveled to the U.S. to interview self-confessed sex addicts—it's just that to frame the film's events, or the characters' actions, particularly Brandon Sullivan's, around this fact feels so . . . inadequate, as though the sex part of sex addiction overshadowed the no less dramatic aspects of addiction: obsession, ruin, withdrawal, depression; obsession, ruin, repetition, relapse.

"We're not bad people. We just come from a bad place." These, the words spoken by the character Sissy (Mulligan) to her brother Brandon (Fassbender), allude to the life before the movie. It's the closest the characters ever get to facing the specter that is the "knowledge-producing event." In other words, something happened to these people, and it happened in the past, that much we can discern, but we are never privy to the particulars of what constitutes the "bad place" to which Sissy refers, yet we can imagine; the characters' actions throughout the film allow us to speculate. In a movie filled with tense moments, this intimate confrontation between brother and sister is no less so. The knowledge of "the bad place," a knowing that Brandon and Sissy share, keeps them bound to one another in ways that surpass my capacity to speak of it. Perhaps because I do not have a brother or, more likely, because I loved and was loved by someone in an unremarkable way, and not always the right way. After, I would often say he felt like my brother, probably because we shared a certain kind of knowing. It shall not be spoken of here.

○

In someone else's memory of that day

○

I was, if not a blessing, then a mistake

○

No one can live in a radically non-narratable world or survive a radically non-narratable life. (Judith Butler)

○

Make room for that (rather than narrative)

○

Calvin Klein, on his mother, Flore: "She'd have white fleece suits lined with black Persian lamb—when you think of the Bronx, you don't think of clothes like that."

○

○

○

Sometimes when H. would ask me what I was feeling, I would reply with a series of movements. These might imitate the gestures of others, their hands wildly intruding upon my face, my eyes, my mouth, my core. H. would suggest it was him to which I was responding—his interest, his questions touching me where I did not want to be touched, until we moved on to the next thought.

○

We fled into what had not yet been written

○

So much of which is private

○

It was neither animal nor element

○

The numbers that represent an item's expiration date.

○

It's just information; how you feel (not who you are);

○

The wish to take something from someone by force.

○

Had something happened to me once? I felt that this knowledge, or lack thereof, structured our silences. When we chose to run towards the nothing rather than to talk. In those moments, I did not feel like who I was because I was too aware that I was being watched, and I had no face apart from this one. Am I writing about loneliness or avoidance (rather than addiction or repulsion)?

○

When I tried to do away with language and long periods without writing commenced, I began to feel sick. Imagine trying to unburden yourself daily of a secret that is not really yours to know or to give away. I struggled to write about the holes and their capacity to produce in me a shift.

○

We threw ourselves against an unknowable form

○

the object that I could not touch

○

from my body it was ~~torn~~ BORN

○

Is this a book about the thing from which I ran
rather than the one I had been running towards

○

According to Judith Butler, to force someone to speak in a manner
that does not honor improvisation, or the unconscious, is to do a
violence to that person. In these instances, we may also unknow-
ingly perpetuate a violence we have already committed against
ourselves. In John Cassavetes's 1977 film, *Opening Night,* an
actress named Myrtle Gordon (performed by the inimitable Gena
Rowlands), is preparing for the Broadway premier of the play-
within-the-play, *The Second Woman,* but struggles to act her part
as everyone else in the film insists she must. As her behavior
becomes increasingly erratic, it becomes difficult to distinguish
whether Myrtle's gradual undoing is an effect of her circum-
stances, or an inevitable byproduct of the actress's process.
Depending on my mood, I sometimes envy not so much Myrtle's
stardom as her ability to improvise and, as a "professional," to
embrace what is unpredictable and not knowable in advance: what
falls outside narrative, as well as that which cannot be subdued to
narrative ends.

○

On the underside of a trapdoor I write the words:

Why not submit
to that which in
you wants to live
if you can love
what is near you
& feel blessed by
its grace; you can

even write incomplete sentences
and then let them / change shape

○

"I" cannot yet say if all this doing was enough. So how can you
know me without my being threatened by that knowing? I never
lacked the words so much as the ability to make meaningful the
sensations. Their hands plastering me with substrate. Colostrum;
milk; earthquake; magnet.

○

What if what we are is not unbroken

○

We gathered so many marigolds like

○

Belief like light foraging into the word

○

Tell me if you've heard this one before

○

were I to acknowledge you
and shape from that a truth

○

the infrared intelligence: red
chiffon glow of my realness

○

The light upon which I throw myself

○

Against everything that exists, that ever existed

○

The woman seated beside me; her gin and tonic

○

○

○

In one of the ACT UP Oral History Project interviews conducted by Sarah Schulman, artist Zoe Leonard recalls a series of photographs she had taken from the inside of an airplane window en route to a conference in Washington, DC. The images, framed by the recognizable curves of the passenger-seat window, feature cloud forms, sometimes a part of the plane's wing, the earth. They center the sublime and invite contemplation: How high can a person go before choosing to look down? What does it mean to live or to leave this earth? Leonard relates to Schulman that the photographs provoke a certain anxiety because their reason for being, at least in 1989, was not entirely clear ("Why am I doing this work?"). In another interview, she reflects, "I felt guilty and torn. I felt detached—my work was so subtle and abstract, so apolitical on the surface." Are these images of clouds any less a revelation if they are not immediately bound up in what the art world understands as "political"? When she shared the photographs and her feelings about them with her friend, and fellow artist, David Wojnarowicz, Leonard recalls he said something to the effect of, "Don't give up on beauty. . . . The goal is to get through this mess so that we can make beautiful work about clouds and about life and existence." At a time when I felt like my life was falling apart, if I survived, it would be because I too had friends that said just as much.

○

○

○

The frequencies gathered around me, and I saw that it mattered which parts became conjugated.

○

If I did not speak of them, know that it was because I needed to be with my silence.

○

I thought of the things about us that no one could ever take away and the fact that it took years for us to feel the beauty of our mistakes as they moved against us and slowly parted the waves.

# ACKNOWLEDGMENTS

To the many kind friends who helped me see the threads: Daniel Borzutzky, Michelle Boulé, Cathy Linh Che, Lightsey Darst, Joshua Escobar, Daley Farr, Chris Fischbach, Corrine Fitzpatrick, T Fleischmann, Johanna Hedva, Brenda Iijima, Lucy Ives, Justin Jones, Molly Kleiman, Jae Matthews, Tiona Nekkia McClodden, Bryan Plucar, Deborah Ramos, Jared Stanley, Sara Jane Stoner, Stacey Tran, Carla Valadez, Aldrin Valdez, Emily Wang, and A. M. Whitehead.

Without the support of the McKnight Foundation, the Jerome Foundation, CantoMundo, Coffee House Press, the Loft, and Marble House Project, this work would have not been possible. Thank you.

This book was written in tandem with a series of blog posts about the Bronx circa 1980 as part of Coffee House Press's In the Stacks residency. Thank you to all the scholars, librarians, artists, and archivists who met with me along the way, and to Annemarie Eayrs and Timothy Otte for coordinating. For those interested in reading on, the posts are available here: https://coffeehousepress .org/blogs/chp-in-the-stacks.

Grateful to Shandaken: Storm King for providing me with a residency opportunity in June 2018 where I began *THRESHOLES,* and to my friends and family at Triple Canopy who kept me sharp.

Some of the writing that appears here was first published in "The Bronx: A Bibliography," as part of *Poor Claudia*'s Ten Sources series, back in 2015.

To the writers whose books touched this text: Etel Adnan, Mei-mei Berssenbrugge, Anne Boyer, Melissa Buzzeo, Anne Carson, Dolores Dorantes, Lyn Hejinian, Susan Howe, Bhanu Kapil, Wayne Koestenbaum, Carole Maso, Nathanaël, Lisa Robertson, Cecilia Vicuña, Rosmarie Waldrop, and C. D. Wright.

I wrote this book for everyone I have ever loved, but probably for Ernie and Raf today above all.

This project was made possible
through generous support from

THE FRINGE FOUNDATION

LITERATURE
is not the same thing as
PUBLISHING

# Funder Acknowledgments

Coffee House Press is an internationally renowned independent book publisher and arts nonprofit based in Minneapolis, MN; through its literary publications and *Books in Action* program, Coffee House acts as a catalyst and connector—between authors and readers, ideas and resources, creativity and community, inspiration and action.

Coffee House Press books are made possible through the generous support of grants and donations from corporations, state and federal grant programs, family foundations, and the many individuals who believe in the transformational power of literature. This activity is made possible by the voters of Minnesota through a Minnesota State Arts Board Operating Support grant, thanks to the legislative appropriation from the Arts and Cultural Heritage Fund. Coffee House also receives major operating support from the Amazon Literary Partnership, Jerome Foundation, McKnight Foundation, Target Foundation, and the National Endowment for the Arts (NEA). To find out more about how NEA grants impact individuals and communities, visit www.arts.gov.

Coffee House Press receives additional support from the Elmer L. & Eleanor J. Andersen Foundation; the David & Mary Anderson Family Foundation; Bookmobile; Dorsey & Whitney LLP; Foundation Technologies; Fredrikson & Byron, P.A.; the Fringe Foundation; Kenneth Koch Literary Estate; the Matching Grant Program Fund of the Minneapolis Foundation; Mr. Pancks' Fund in memory of Graham Kimpton; the Schwab Charitable Fund; Schwegman, Lundberg & Woessner, P.A.; the Silicon Valley Community Foundation; and the U.S. Bank Foundation.

## The Publisher's Circle of Coffee House Press

Publisher's Circle members make significant contributions to Coffee House Press's annual giving campaign. Understanding that a strong financial base is necessary for the press to meet the challenges and opportunities that arise each year, this group plays a crucial part in the success of Coffee House's mission.

Recent Publisher's Circle members include many anonymous donors, Suzanne Allen, Patricia A. Beithon, the E. Thomas Binger & Rebecca Rand Fund of the Minneapolis Foundation, Andrew Brantingham, Robert & Gail Buuck, Dave & Kelli Cloutier, Louise Copeland, Jane Dalrymple-Hollo & Stephen Parlato, Mary Ebert & Paul Stembler, Kaywin Feldman & Jim Lutz, Chris Fischbach & Katie Dublinski, Sally French, Jocelyn Hale & Glenn Miller, the Rehael Fund-Roger Hale/Nor Hall of the Minneapolis Foundation, Randy Hartten & Ron Lotz, Dylan Hicks & Nina Hale, William Hardacker, Randall Heath, Jeffrey Hom, Carl & Heidi Horsch, the Amy L. Hubbard & Geoffrey J. Kehoe Fund, Kenneth & Susan Kahn, Stephen & Isabel Keating, Julia Klein, the Kenneth Koch Literary Estate, Cinda Kornblum, Jennifer Kwon Dobbs & Stefan Liess, the Lambert Family Foundation, the Lenfestey Family Foundation, Joy Linsday Crow, Sarah Lutman & Rob Rudolph, the Carol & Aaron Mack Charitable Fund of the Minneapolis Foundation, George & Olga Mack, Joshua Mack & Ron Warren, Gillian McCain, Malcolm S. McDermid & Katie Windle, Mary & Malcolm McDermid, Sjur Midness & Briar Andresen, Daniel N. Smith III & Maureen Millea Smith, Peter Nelson & Jennifer Swenson, Enrique & Jennifer Olivarez, Alan Polsky, Marc Porter & James Hennessy, Robin Preble, Alexis Scott, Ruth Stricker Dayton, Jeffrey Sugerman & Sarah Schultz, Nan G. Swid, Kenneth Thorp in memory of Allan Kornblum & Rochelle Ratner, Patricia Tilton, Joanne Von Blon, Stu Wilson & Melissa Barker, Warren D. Woessner & Iris C. Freeman, and Margaret Wurtele.

For more information about the Publisher's Circle and other ways to support Coffee House Press books, authors, and activities, please visit www.coffeehousepress.org/pages/support or contact us at info@coffeehousepress.org.

LARA MIMOSA MONTES is a writer based in Minneapolis and New York. Her poems and essays have appeared in the Academy of American Poets' Poem-a-Day series, *BOMB, Boston Review, Jacket2,* and elsewhere. She is a 2018 McKnight Writing Fellow and CantoMundo Fellow. She holds a PhD in English from the Graduate Center, City University of New York. Currently, she works as a senior editor of *Triple Canopy.* She was born in the Bronx.

*THRESHOLES* was designed by
Bookmobile Design & Digital Publisher Services.
Text is set in Minion Pro.

CPSIA information can be obtained
at www.ICGtesting.com
Printed in the USA
JSHW081918090623
42855JS00001B/2